better together*

* This book is best read together, grownup and kid.

 akidsco.com

a
kids
book
about

a kids book about

CIVIC ENGAGEMENT

by Marissa Grass

A Kids Co.
Editor Emma Wolf
Designer Rick DeLucco
Creative Director Rick DeLucco
Studio Manager Kenya Feldes
Sales Director Melanie Wilkins
Head of Books Jennifer Goldstein
CEO and Founder Jelani Memory

DK
Delhi Technical Team Bimlesh Tiwary Pushpak Tyagi, Rakesh Kumar
Senior Production Editor Jennifer Murray
Senior Production Controller Louise Minihane
Senior Acquisitions Editor Katy Flint
Acquisitions Project Editor Sara Forster
Managing Art Editor Vicky Short
Managing Director, Licensing Mark Searle

First American edition, 2025
Published in the United States by DK Publishing, 1745 Broadway, 20th Floor,
New York, NY 10019

First published in Great Britain in 2025 by
Dorling Kindersley Limited, 20 Vauxhall Bridge Road, London SW1V 2SA
A Penguin Random House Company

The authorised representative in the EEA is
Dorling Kindersley Verlag GmbH. Arnulfstr. 124, 80636 Munich, Germany

A catalog record for this book is available from the Library of Congress.
A CIP catalogue record for this book is available from the British Library.
ISBN: 978-0-5939-7037-9

DK books are available at special discounts when purchased in bulk for sales
promotions, premiums, fund-raising, or education use. For details, contact:
DK Publishing Special Markets, 1745 Broadway, 20th Floor, New York, NY 10019
SpecialSales@dk.com

Printed and bound in China
www.dk.com
akidsco.com

This book was made with Forest
Stewardship Council™ certified
paper – one small step in DK's
commitment to a sustainable future.
Learn more at www.dk.com/uk/
information/sustainability

This book is dedicated to kids
everywhere, especially the ones I love.

Most of all, for Theo and Cora.

Intro
for grownups

I wrote this book as an invitation to dream. What we know and believe about government—who it serves, how it functions, and where decisions get made—can change. And, it feels imperative that kids lead the way.

What we need are fresh, innovative ideas, and kids have no shortage of them! They are great at learning new things, thinking creatively about problems, including others, and advocating for compromise.

Plus, so many of the decisions about things that kids care about—parks, schools, and other activities—are made locally.

This book is for you as much as it is for the person you are reading it with. I hope you'll accept this invitation to dream right alongside them about what our world can be.

If you could change one thing about the place you live, what would it be?

One thing in

YOUR NEIGHBORHOOD,

YOUR SCHOOL,

OR YOUR CITY?

How about this: what's something about your community you really

VE?

MAYBE

it's a special park in your neighborhood.

it's a special program at your library.

it's a special event your school puts on every year.

Do you know what all of these things have in common?

THEY'RE ALL CREATED BY PEOPLE IN YOUR COMMUNITY.

And you can be one of them!

How?

Through something called

CIVIC ENGAGEMENT.

What's that?

It's how you can make a difference in your community.

It's choosing to be a part of how decisions are made.

It's being involved in the day-to-day happenings of where you live.

"CIVIC"

means relating to
a city or town.

"ENGAGEMENT"

means being involved
or doing something.

And anybody within a community can get directly involved with how their community grows and changes— this is **civic engagement**.

IN FACT,

I believe that civic engagement is important for *everybody*!

And I especially believe
that it's important for kids.

Why is that?

YOUR VOICE MATTERS.

Important decisions are made
every day about your community.

And these decisions impact
YOU, YOUR FRIENDS, AND YOUR FAMILY.

HERE'S A QUESTION:

What comes to mind when
you think about government?

Many people think of it as something big, distant, or difficult to understand.

But I'll tell you a secret...

That's something silly a lot of grownups believe! I know *you* know better.

Government is actually people right here, in your community, who are working to make a difference every day.

They can be...

your neighbor,

your librarian,

your school principal,

maybe even your grownups!

And they make decisions
which impact all different
parts of the community.

Some decisions are made in your city, your region, your state, and even Washington, DC!

And those decisions impact...

the water you drink,

the parks in your neighborhood,

the books in your library,

the roads we drive on,

public transportation,

what happens when you flush the toilet,

and lots of other things!

THERE'S SOMETHING BIG I WANT YOU TO KNOW.

Seriously, you won't
want to miss this!

The most important part
of these decisions...

IS YO

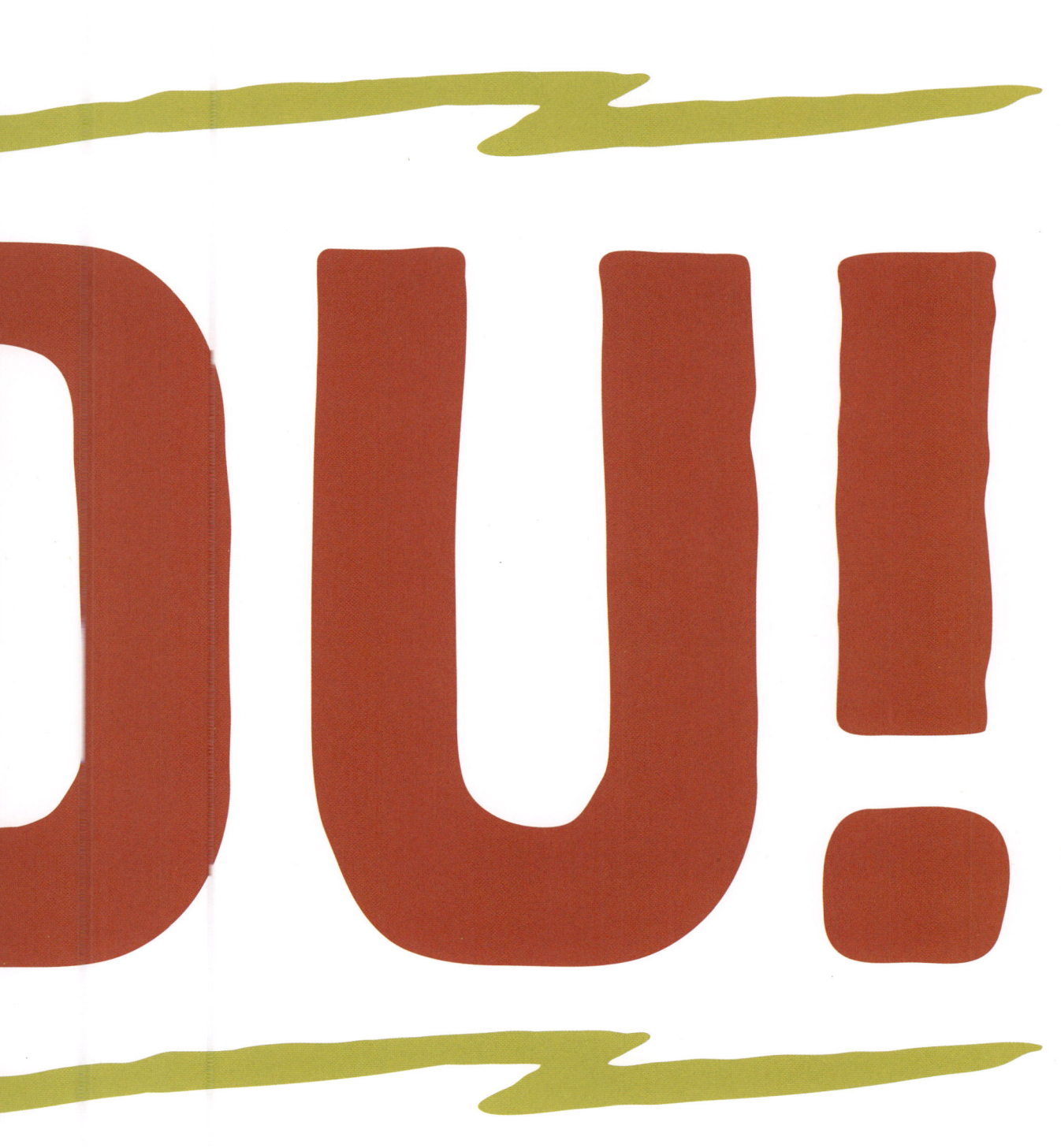

We elect people to represent us and advocate for what we need.

And what you need and want to see happen in your community matters.

A person has to be 18 to vote, but your government officials represent everyone, regardless of age.

You are a vital piece of your community, and what you think is important.

SO, WHAT MATTERS TO YOU?

WHAT DO YOU CARE ABOUT?

If you could change something about your community, what would it be?

I want you to pause here and really think about it.

Turn the page when you're ready, but no rush!

What came to mind for you?

What ideas do you have to
make your community better?

Civic engagement is all about doing something with those ideas.

What can that look like?

VOLUNTEER.

Make a meal to share, donate, take care of the environment, and lend a hand where you can.

There are lots of ways to donate your time and resources.

WRITE.

Write letters to your representatives about issues which matter to you, or respond to surveys to share your thoughts about important projects.

ATTEND AN EVENT.

Join in on town hall discussions, neighborhood meetings, or open houses for community projects.

USE
YOUR
VOICE.

Call your representatives or sign up to testify* in a city council or school board meeting.

*This means speaking to the elected leaders about a particular issue you care about. Local leaders love when kids testify!

CIVIC ENGAGEMENT

is like a muscle—it gets stronger the more you use it.

It also prepares you for when you can vote or run for government positions yourself!

ONE DAY, your generation will be the people in power, making all of the decisions.

And we need kind, compassionate, smart people like you leading the way toward better communities.

Share your story with local officials, and encourage your family and friends to get involved.

CIVIC ENGAGEMENT IS FOR ALL OF US.

EVERY

CAN M

DIFFE

YBODY
AKE A
RENCE!

Outro
for grownups

So, what's next? This book is meant to start conversations between kids and grownups about what they need to grow up happy and healthy. My ask of grownups is to be fierce advocates for the things that are important to your kids.

- Listen when they share what matters most to them.

- Research ways to get involved or speak out on an issue that is meaningful to you and/ or your kid(s).

- Set goals and define your ask: What specific action can elected leaders take on issues you care about?

- Build relationships with community leaders.

- Take action—model community engagement for and with your kids.

Let us all find ways to amplify their voices.

Thank you.

About The Author

Marissa Grass (she/her) wrote this book for kids who want to change the world.

Her career in local government spans areas such as city planning, utilities, garbage and recycling, emergency management, and parks and recreation.

Marissa ran for class president in 8th grade because of her belief that individual action, collectively, is what will change the world.

This book is a blueprint for how to do just that, and (spoiler alert!) you don't have to be a grownup to do it. Kids all over the world are inspiring action every day—where will you start?

 @marissa.grass   🌐 www.marissagrass.com

Made to empower.

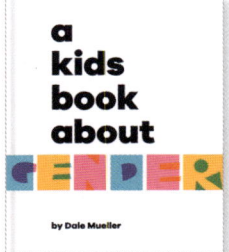

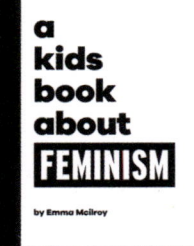
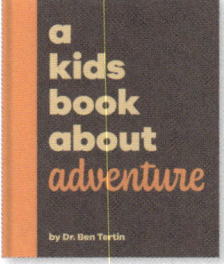
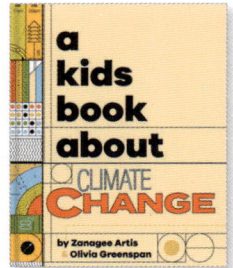

Discover more at akidsco.com